Words to Work By

31 devotions for the workplace based on the Book of Proverbs

Jacquelyn Lynn

Words to Work By
31 devotions for the workplace based on the Book of Proverbs

Jacquelyn Lynn

Publisher: Tuscawilla Creative Services, LLC
Cover Design: Jerry D. Clement
Photography: Jerry D. Clement
Interior Design and Production: Tuscawilla Creative Services, LLC

ISBN: 978-0-9853208-2-9

For bulk purchasing information, email info@contactTCS.com

Tuscawilla Creative Services LLC
P. O. Box 1501
Goldenrod, FL 32733-1501
www.tuscawillacreativeservices.com

Contents

For Jerry
because words are not enough

Words to Work By

31 devotions for the workplace based on the Book of Proverbs

The wisest king to rule Israel, Solomon, wrote much of *Proverbs* to show how Godly wisdom merges with day-to-day life. Though Solomon reigned in the tenth century B.C., his words are as applicable and useful today as they were more than 3,000 years ago. In fact, *Proverbs* has been called the best business book ever written. With 31 chapters, the book itself is a perfect devotional: Just read one chapter a day and start over each month. As scripture always does, it will speak to you differently each time.

To write *Words to Work By*, I studied the *Book of Proverbs*, selected a single verse from each chapter, and wrote devotions based on what those verses said to me. I hope you'll find these messages meaningful in your workplace and beyond.

Peace,

Jacquelyn Lynn

1

Value

Such is the end of all who go after ill-gotten gain; it takes away the lives of those who get it.

Proverbs 1:19

re you stealing from your employer? How about from your customers?

The term *workplace theft* is usually used to describe embezzling money or taking equipment or supplies without permission. But there's another way theft occurs in the business world: When individuals fail to deliver the full value pledged in exchange for the agreed-on compensation.

We tend to think of wages in terms of what the employer pays rather than what the employee provides in exchange for the money. Similarly, we tend to think of products in terms of cost (price) rather than value (worth).

Whether you are an individual selling your labor as an employee, a service provider being paid as an independent contractor, or a business selling a product, at a very minimum you should provide what you promised in exchange for the compensation you receive. To do anything less is to steal from those who are paying you. To do more is a demonstration of your own integrity.

When you steal from others, you rob yourself. When you give less than your best, you erode your sense of self-worth. When you fail to respect and meet your own obligations, you diminish your ultimate value.

But when you refuse to steal, you enrich yourself. When you give your absolute best, you can be confident in your value. When you meet your commitments, you know you have performed with honor.

Those are the gains worth having in life. They create the life God wants us to live.

Dear God,
Please give me the
strength and wisdom to
consistently do Your will
and my best, to exceed
expectations in all my
transactions and
relationships.
Amen

2

Understanding

Discretion will protect you, and understanding will guard you.

Proverbs 2:11

A man with three young children boarded a commuter train, took a seat, bowed his head and covered his eyes. The kids sat quietly for a few moments, then started moving around. It wasn't long before they were running up and down the aisle, laughing and screaming at each other, bumping into other passengers. All the while, their father sat still, apparently ignoring them.

Finally a passenger spoke up. "Excuse me, sir," he said, annoyance obvious in his voice. "Please get your children under control. They're making it impossible for the rest of us to ride in peace."

The man raised his head and stared bleakly at the passenger who had spoken aloud what everyone else on the train was thinking. "I'm sorry," he said. "We just left the hospital where their mother died. I don't know how to tell them and I don't know what to do."

Variations on this story have been circulating for years. It may or may not be true, but the message is important: Before you make a judgment or take action on something involving others, try to understand what's going on in the other person's life that is not immediately evident.

Whether you are a coworker or a supervisor, be slow to criticize or condemn a change in behavior, attitude or performance. External behavior is often just a symptom of more serious underlying circumstances – circumstances that might need anything from just a little time and understanding to some major assistance to work out.

Of course, you have a job to do and a business to run – which is all the more reason for you to seek to understand what is not readily apparent and determine an appropriate course of action. It's good business to do what you can to retain experienced workers, even if it means helping them through a personal rough patch. Whatever you do, be discreet and keep confidences. Repeat nothing without explicit permission. Be someone people can trust to see their side, offer appropriate assistance and protect their privacy.

Dear God,

When someone is having a problem, give me the ability to look below the surface, to see beyond the symptoms to the cause, to understand how to help, and to do it all with the utmost of discretion.

Amen

3

Reward

Do not withhold good from those who deserve it, when it is in your power to act.

Proverbs 3:27

esearch tells us that a primary reason people steal from their employers is because they feel they aren't being adequately compensated through their wages. They don't think they're doing anything wrong because they see what they've stolen as something they're entitled to. Research also tells us that while money is important to workers, it's not the only thing – and often not the top thing – that motivates them.

Years ago, I worked with a supervisor who never uttered a word of thanks or praise to his team. Once I mentioned that one of the junior people could use a few words of appreciation and encouragement, and he said, "He gets his 'appreciation' in his paycheck every week. That's thanks enough." Not long after that, the young man who was only thanked by getting paid accepted a job offer from a competing company – and he took several valuable customers with him. While he was doing essentially the same work, his new employer offered a more prestigious title, a slightly higher wage, advancement opportunities, and recognition for a job well done.

Regardless of where you are in the corporate hierarchy – and indeed in all aspects of your life – don't be stingy with recognition and commendation. Whether you are the janitor or the CEO, when people around you deserve an expression of appreciation or praise, give it to them. It takes just a few seconds to say, "Good job," or to send an email or IM that says, "Thanks for what you did."

Don't limit your thanks and praise to colleagues and subordinates – the president of the company can use a little positive reinforcement every now and then, too!

If you control wages, be as generous as possible with base salary, bonuses and benefits while still being fiscally responsible. From a very practical perspective, you'll see less turnover and greater loyalty on your staff. Even more important is that you'll be running your operation the way God wants you to.

Dear God,
Keep me alert to
opportunities to be
generous with those I
work with. Help me
notice the good they do
and recognize it with my
own words and deeds.
Amen

4

Consistency

Get wisdom, get understanding; do not forget my words or swerve from them.

Proverbs 4:5

A woman was driving too fast, changing lanes quickly, tailgating the cars in front of her and making ugly gestures to drivers that didn't get out of her way. When the police officer saw her, he called for backup before pulling her over. She was shocked when her minivan was suddenly surrounded by police cars with lights flashing and tense officers ready to pull their weapons.

As she produced her license and registration, she asked the lead officer why it took so much police power to conduct one simple traffic stop. "I thought for sure your car had been stolen," he said. "You've got a bumper sticker that says 'Follow me to church' and another that says 'Proud to be a Christian.' I didn't think anyone who would put those bumper stickers on a car would be driving the way you were."

Okay, that's a joke that's gone around the internet for years. But in addition to the irony, there's probably some truth to it.

God does not want us to limit the time we practice our faith to the hour or so we spend at church in worship every week. He wants us to live as He has told us every minute of every day. He wants us to be strong, positive representatives of all of His children in the world. We can only do that if we know what He has said, which is why He wants us to study His Word (the Bible) and follow His commands.

Is this easy? No. It takes time, energy and effort to read and understand scripture. And it takes strength and discipline to live a Godly life in a world that is full of temptation and frustration. But the good news is that all the help you need to know and apply the fundamentals of scripture is readily available – just ask God and He will provide it. He will give you the wisdom and the resources you need to live the life He has planned for you, whether you are at work, at play, at church or anywhere else.

Dear God,

As I go through the day,

keep me close to You, let

me hear You in my head

and my heart, so that I

might live out Your will for

my life minute by minute

in all of my actions and

thoughts.

Amen

5

Transparency

For a man's ways are in full view of the LORD, and he examines all his paths.

Proverbs 5:21

When I was a little girl and going through a stage of extreme modesty and prissiness, I was appalled when I realized that God could see me when I was in the bathroom. It was a struggle to balance the concept that God was watching and caring for me all the time with the idea that He could see me doing something so private and, well, so icky.

As an adult, knowing that God sees and knows everything – even what happens in the bathroom! – provides me with incalculable comfort and security.

Even though God is the only one who sees absolutely everything, in today's high-tech world, others have a pretty big window into our lives. Through the internet and social media, we have opened up in ways that previous generations could not imagine. What a wonderful opportunity to share our faith through our actions!

Does this mean your corporate website should include sermons and your personal and/or company Facebook or LinkedIn updates should include scripture? Not necessarily. A better strategy is to live your life personally and professionally according to God's commands and let others see you doing it.

As St. Francis of Assisi said: "Preach the gospel always; if necessary, use words." Do the right thing because it's the right thing, whether it's delivering a quality product or service at a fair price, responding promptly to a complaint, honoring your commitments or simply refusing to gossip. When you make a mistake, take responsibility and make it right. And remember to give graciously and generously without calculating the return.

Good or bad, our world is evolving into one with less and less privacy. Use this evolution to demonstrate to an ever-broadening audience the joy of living the life God wants for you.

Dear God,

You see me clearly – far more clearly than I see myself. Thank You for being with me every moment and for helping me to be a reflection of Your love.

Amen

6

Harmony

... the Lord hates ... a false witness who pours out lies and a man who stirs up dissension among brothers.

Proverbs 6:16, 19

Healthy competition can be good for an organization. Humans are competitive creatures – some more than others – and we all like to win. But there is a huge difference between encouraging healthy competition and pitting one person against another.

Reality shows like *Survivor*, *The Apprentice*, and even *The Bachelor* often portray competition that goes far beyond healthy to cut-throat, and the conduct of those characters often finds its way into our workplaces and even personal lives. And some managers seem to encourage that. In fact, a lot of business leaders think that benchmarking workers against each other will encourage them to work harder, either to retain their high ranking or raise a lower one. In most cases, the results are the opposite: the leaders may not see any reason to work harder because they're already on top and low-ranking workers can get discouraged and stop trying. And in some cases, workers will resort to unethical tactics to achieve a desired ranking.

What really hurts the organization is that when people are focused on internal competition, their relationships with their coworkers suffer and they often lose sight of the company's overall performance goals.

There are no corporate results that can justify dishonesty or deliberately generating discord. At work, as in the local church, God wants us to remain part of the Body of Christ, to understand our individual contributions and to use them in concert with the gifts of others. He wants us to serve our coworkers and customers in ways that glorify Him – and that means to work to the best of our ability in truth and harmony with one another.

Dear God,
Guide my head and heart
as I set my goals and
develop a plan to reach
them. Help me make that
plan worthy of You.
Amen

7

Obedience

*Keep my commands and you will live; guard
my teachings as the apple of your eye.*

Proverbs 7:2

I participate in an online networking group of entrepreneurs and business leaders. When someone posed the question of how to run a Christian business, the discussion splintered into two primary directions. Some people talked about principles and practices; others focused on whether there could even be such a thing as a Christian business.

A business does not have the capacity to be Christian – or not. It is the people within that business who might be Christians, Jews, Muslims, Wiccans or part of any other faith group or no faith group at all. And it's the faith a company's owners and employees embrace that likely guides their conduct at work.

It's not unusual for a company's culture to be based on the faith of its owners. For example, Chick-fil-A's corporate purpose is: "To glorify God by being a faithful steward of all that is entrusted to us. To have a positive influence on all who come in contact with Chick-fil-A." The company is famous for staying closed on Sundays so that employees have an opportunity to rest, spend time with family and friends, and worship if they choose to do so.

Does a commitment to run a company or even simply do one's job according to God's commands guarantee profitability and worldly success? No. It is, however, pleasing to God and there is no greater goal than that.

We are the center of God's attention, the focus of His vision. He sees us all the time – He doesn't turn His head when we go to work. God is not like a boss or colleague who might praise certain performance but look the other way when corners are being cut. God's watchfulness is much like a parent sitting on the edge of the playground as children play. He's there, seeing everything, appreciating that His commands are being followed, grieving when they are not, and ready to step in when one of His children needs help and calls for Him.

There may be times when we are out of view of other

humans, but we are always in full view of God. God wants us to live and work according to His purpose, and He loves watching us do it. Even better is that He shares His joy by enriching our lives—not necessarily in material ways, but with a fullness of life we cannot otherwise experience.

Dear God,
Your commands are
exactly what I need. Help
me know and follow Your
commands every minute
of every day, no matter
where I am, what I am
doing, or who can see me.
Amen

8

Knowledge

*Choose my instruction instead of silver,
knowledge rather than choice gold, for wisdom
is more precious than rubies, and nothing you
desire can compare with her.*

Proverbs 8:10-11

B ack in 2007 and 2008, some friends of mine were the epitome of the American dream. Between his career in the financial services industry and her consulting business, their income was in the upper six figures. They weren't ostentatious, but they lived in an upscale home, drove luxury cars, dressed well, and made generous contributions to their

church and other charities.

Then the Great Recession hit. He lost his job; she lost more than half of her clients. Their income dropped to maybe 10 percent of what it had been. Suddenly they were facing challenges they had never expected.

They weren't alone. Millions of people were struggling with similar circumstances. But my friends were grounded in their faith. They knew God's Word and they trusted the Lord. They had lost money and material things, but they had knowledge and integrity. Together, they shifted professional gears, used what they had learned and rebuilt her consulting business to meet the needs of a changing market. They honored their financial obligations and are once again enjoying a comfortable lifestyle.

Worldly possessions come and go. We can lose them through no fault of our own – or by our own devices. But wisdom, once gained, is ours to keep, and when coupled with integrity is far more valuable than any amount of money.

Dear God,
I came into this world
with nothing and will go
out with nothing – except
the amazing richness of
Your love and promise of
everlasting life. Please
help me to always choose
You over worldly
treasures.
Amen

9

Wisdom

Do not rebuke a mocker or he will hate you;
rebuke a wise man and he will love you.
Instruct a wise man and he will be wiser still;
teach a righteous man and he will add to his
learning.

Proverbs 9:8-9

About 25 drivers were employed at a city terminal of a national trucking company. Of those drivers, one was responsible for fueling all the vehicles and moving tractors and trailers around the freight yard as necessary. He rarely drove a truck out on the street to make deliveries.

A new operations manager came on board, determined to make his mark. He decided that the drivers could fuel their own vehicles and whoever was available could handle staging the equipment, which would increase the number of drivers on the street – and, he thought, improve service.

Several of the senior drivers tried to explain why that approach was not as efficient as the way it was being done. Not only did the manager refuse to listen, he was openly scornful.

When his plan was implemented, productivity dropped, service suffered, costs increased and grievances were filed. Eventually upper management was forced to step in. The operations manager resigned and was replaced with a leader who not only treated the drivers (and everyone else) with respect, but appreciated the fact that they knew things he didn't.

When the new manager saw a problem, he went to the people involved and collaborated on a solution. And he genuinely welcomed differing opinions.

The smartest people are the ones who aren't afraid to say, "I don't know." They're not reluctant to ask for help. And they appreciate every opportunity to learn.

Wise people welcome instruction, education and yes, even correction. They're grateful when someone stops them from making a mistake or helps them correct an error they made – and wise people are not too proud to admit that they don't always get it right. They know that only God knows it all and that God often speaks to us through the mouths and actions of others. To learn, we have to listen – listen with discernment, certainly, but listen.

Dear God,
Thank You for sending the
greatest teacher of all:
Jesus. Help me to always
love my teachers in
whatever form they
appear, to never stop
learning and to use my
knowledge in Your service.
Amen

10

Integrity

When words are many, sin is not absent, but
he who holds his tongue is wise.

Proverbs 10:19

Have you ever listened to someone, heard every word but didn't understand, and then felt like you were the dumb one because you didn't get it?

A client – the founder and CEO of a $250 million company – once asked me to sit in on an interview the executive team of his company was conducting with a candidate for the position of marketing director. The man had an impressive resume. He spoke rapidly and with great confidence – and he certainly knew all the marketing buzzwords. But after more than an hour of listening to him, I wasn't sure what he was saying.

When the interview was over, my client asked me what I thought of him. I qualified my answer by pointing out that I hadn't been involved in the earlier screening and it was possible the reason I didn't understand much of what he said was because I didn't have the proper information foundation. And then I told the truth: "He sounded good while he was talking, but now that I'm out of the room and thinking about it, I'm not really sure what he said."

My client laughed and admitted, "I don't have a clue what he said, but he must be smarter than I am about marketing."

The man was hired – and it turned out to be a huge mistake. He didn't know how to manage a creative team; he was scornful of customers and rude to subordinates; he lacked communication and interpersonal skills; it didn't bother him a bit to sacrifice others to protect himself; and his sense of ethics was, at best, questionable. But he always sounded good.

You cannot cover up or explain wrongdoing by talking a lot. The ability to speak well and do it at length does not necessarily mean what the speaker is saying has value. W.C. Fields is credited with saying, "If you can't dazzle them with brilliance, baffle them with [nonsense]."

God does not want us to baffle anyone. He wants us to speak with wisdom and clarity – and to be silent in the same way.

Dear God,

**Help me communicate
with truth and accuracy.
Give me the words to
speak so that I may be
clearly understood and
the wisdom to know when
to stay silent.**

Amen

11

Generosity

A generous man will prosper; he who refreshes others will himself be refreshed.

Proverbs 11:25

One of the most exciting aspects of our time is social media and the spotlight it has put on giving.

I'm not talking about tithing to the church, feeding the hungry or clothing the poor. Nor am I talking about companies that make charitable contributions for which their logos are prominently displayed in a variety of places. Those things are all good, but they've been around for a long time.

Social media or the social web is one of the best illustrations of how what you give comes back to you – and how not giving can bite you. Companies that are successfully using social media are generously putting a significant amount of quality content on their websites (their own corporate sites and their social media pages) that people can access at no charge. They're offering free advice, information, entertainment and assistance. Certainly they're not doing this in a spirit of total altruism – they want and need customers. But they know that engaging by giving quality content and service before they try to sell their product is the way to achieve online success. They first give, and when they do, it comes back to them multifold.

Did Mark Zuckerberg have any idea that Facebook would become such a Biblical platform for people and companies? I doubt it. What about Reid Hoffman, the founder of LinkedIn? Again, not likely. But God has a way of working through people in ways that we often don't expect. God wants us to give – which is why He provides us the vehicles by which we can do it and the rewards for our efforts.

Dear God,
Keep me focused on giving not for gain but because that is Your will for me. Help me to be the cheerful giver that You love, to never miss an opportunity to be the generous person You have called me to be.

Amen

12

Honesty

Better to be a nobody and yet have a servant
than pretend to be somebody and have no food.

Proverbs 12:9

When I was in my 20s, I met a man who was attractive, articulate and interesting, so when he invited me to dinner, I accepted. It was our first and last date.

There was a waiting list at the restaurant, and when the hostess asked for his name, he said, "Dr. Reynolds." I don't recall now what he did for a living, but he wasn't a doctor. When I questioned him, he responded: "It impresses them. We'll get seated faster and get better service."

As best I could tell, we were seated in the order we arrived. The service was good, but the restaurant was upscale and had an excellent reputation so I don't think we were treated any differently because he claimed to be a doctor. When the bill came, he paid in cash and didn't leave a tip. I was sure it was an oversight and called it to his attention. He said he worked hard for his money and wasn't going to waste it on tipping a server, and it didn't seem to bother him that servers depend on tips for their income.

He seemed surprised when I declined a second date.

I would have been happier – and would have seen him again – had he taken me to a less expensive restaurant, skipped the doctor charade and left a fair tip for the server.

We live in a world where people are often judged by their material achievements, so it's tempting to put up a façade. But living that kind of lie only leaves you empty. When we are able to be authentic and honest, our lives are far richer than when we are pretending to be something we're not and have things we don't.

God has a plan for each of us. While the plan He has for you is not the same as the plan He has for anyone else, all of God's plans share His command for honesty and integrity. Nowhere is that more important than in our business dealings. If we have to show off, if we have to pretend to be something that we're not, we're probably not living God's plan – and we're certainly not building our professional lives on a solid foundation that will serve us over the years.

Dear God,
Thank you for making me
who I am, and for loving
me so much that You
want me to grow and
mature in Your ways. And
thank you for helping me
stay honest, because the
truth is the most delicious
meal we can ever eat.
Amen

13

Humility

Pride only breeds quarrels, but wisdom is found in those who take advice.

Proverbs 13:10

A CEO of a pharmaceutical company was challenged by conflict among his senior leadership team. He was considering replacing one or more members of the team when someone suggested that he might first want to ask those subordinates for coaching. At first he resisted – he was, after all, the top dog. Then, with great reluctance, he decided to give it a try.

It wasn't easy for the CEO or for the subordinates, who weren't sure he truly wanted sincere feedback. When they finally opened up, the CEO received some surprising but useful information. He learned that he was perceived as a poor listener who didn't care what others thought. While the company's executives thought the CEO was a brilliant strategist and creative thinker, they also saw him as an ineffective manager and leader.

The CEO immediately began the challenging task of responding to the advice he had sought. He learned to reach out to his direct reports for information and guidance, and he encouraged them to do the same with their subordinates. He made a conscious effort to ask more questions, listen more and talk less, and share more of his own concerns and issues. In the process, he realized that asking for advice and coaching was a sign of strength, not of weakness.

No matter how much you know, there will always be more to learn. Open your eyes and your heart to the abundance of teachers God has placed in your world who are waiting to share what they know.

Dear God,

**Help me to remember
that when You speak, it is
often through
circumstances or other
people. Let me never be
too proud to learn from
others, no matter what
their rank or position.**

Amen

14

Reconciliation

Fools mock at making amends for sin, but goodwill is found among the upright.

Proverbs 14:9

Public figures are masters at the non-apology. It usually goes like this: "If anyone was hurt or offended by what I said or did, I am sorry." It reminds me of the line in the classic *Gone With the Wind*, where Rhett tells Scarlett she's like the thief who is not sorry he stole, but is very sorry he got caught. When you hear a non-apology, you're hearing that the person isn't really sorry for what he did, he's sorry that he's having to deal with negative consequences.

When we do something wrong that hurts someone else, the best thing we can do is make sincere amends and work to restore the relationship. We won't always succeed, but that's okay – the point is to try and know that we made an honest effort. Sometimes a genuine apology is all that's needed; other times, some restitution may be in order.

We can all learn from the Jewish holiday of Yom Kippur (Day of Atonement) – the holiest day of the Jewish year. Atonement means reconciliation, as in bringing together those who have been separated by some act. Look at the construction of the word: *at-one-ment*. Yom Kippur addresses the reconciliation of humans with God, but we can take that concept into our human relationships because God wants us to reconcile with each other. When we resolve our conflicts, we often build relationships that are stronger than they were before the problem occurred.

Sometimes the hardest part of reconciliation is forgiving ourselves. Keep this in mind: God forgives all of our sins. There is nothing we can do that God won't forgive if we truly repent. If God can forgive us, how can we do less for ourselves?

Dear God,

Your unconditional love
and forgiveness is the best
model we can follow for
our human relationships.
Thank You for giving me
the strength and insight to
truly make amends and
achieve reconciliation with
anyone I have harmed.

Amen

15

Respect

*Better a meal of vegetables where there is love
than a fattened calf with hatred.*

Proverbs 15:17

ost of us work for the money. We
may enjoy our jobs to varying degrees,
but we work for the money so that we
can buy the necessities we need and even some
of the luxuries we want. Still, work is not *all*
about the money. It's about satisfaction in a job
well done, serving our customers with integrity
and working in an environment of harmony and
mutual respect.

Smart business leaders build a culture of caring, genuine teamwork and ethical values. They compensate their employees as fairly and competitively as possible, understanding that compensation includes far more than the numbers on a pay stub. And at the first signs of discord and dissention, they move swiftly to identify and address the troublesome issues.

We don't have to be best friends with everyone we work with. In fact, it's probably better if we're not. But we have to be able to eat with those people – both figuratively and literally – without our stomachs getting tied up in knots of anger and anxiety.

Dear God,
You meet our every need –
and often many of our
wants. Help me to trust
that You will provide for
me in accordance with
Your plan. If I am not
working where and how
You want me to be, guide
me so I can get back on
Your track.
Amen

16

Responsibility

A wise man's heart guides his mouth, and his lips promote instruction.

Proverbs 16:23

In my career before I started writing professionally, I was a sales rep for a major trucking company. The company hired a young man for its management training program and assigned him to the terminal where I worked. He was just out of college, smart and confident to the point of being cocky – and we clashed almost from day one. A couple of months into his six-month training program, our relationship had progressed from politely cool to openly hostile.

One afternoon, he came into my office and asked if we could talk. He closed the door, sat down, took a deep breath and said, "I don't know how things got to this point, but we have a problem and I want to fix it."

Showing wisdom beyond his years, he went on to take full responsibility for our conflict – even though we both knew that we were equally to blame. He said that he liked and respected me, and knew that he could learn a lot from me.

Johann Wolfgang von Goethe said, "If you treat an individual as if he were what he ought to be and could be, he will become what he ought to be and could be." One of my many mistakes in that whole scenario was that I didn't treat this young man like the professional he had the potential to become. I thought he was arrogant and I wanted to take him down a notch or two. Maybe I did, but I brought myself down at the same time.

He did what I, as the senior person in the relationship, should have done. (Actually, as the senior person, I should have never allowed the situation to deteriorate to the point that it had.) And yes, over the next few months, we became friends and he did learn a lot from me – but I learned more from him.

Perhaps the biggest lesson for both of us was: Listen to your heart before engaging your mouth.

Dear God,

As Your children, we are all works in progress, maturing every day. Thank you for all of the opportunities you give me to both learn and teach, because in teaching I learn, and learning helps me become a better teacher.

Amen

17

Discretion

*Even a fool is thought wise if he keeps silent,
and discerning if he holds his tongue.*

Proverbs 17:28

A lot has been written about the value in keeping quiet. One saying goes, "Do not speak unless you can improve the silence." The Greek philosopher Epictetus said, "We have two ears and one mouth so that we can listen twice as much as we speak." Abraham Lincoln is credited with having said, "Better to remain silent and be thought a fool than to speak out and remove all doubt." Obviously, Mr.

Lincoln was inspired by a writer who penned a similar sentiment about 3,000 years ago.

On a less philosophical note, I have heard more than one sales trainer say, "Ask a question, then shut up. The person who speaks first loses." Business discussions of all kinds – especially sales conversations – should not be about winning and losing, but the point of staying quiet and giving the other person the opportunity to talk is important.

Though there are many situations when silence is appropriate (for example, when a friend needs a sounding board), two key times you should be silent in the workplace are:

1. When you want information.

2. When you are not absolutely certain about what you are thinking of saying.

When you don't speak, you give others the opportunity to share what they know and you don't risk saying the wrong thing. It sounds so simple, and yet we so often feel compelled to jump in and fill up silence with noise. Before you speak, count to ten in your head and then ask God what He would have you say. Don't be surprised when the answer is, "Nothing."

Our basic biology (two ears, two eyes, one mouth) along with Biblical wisdom and practical experience all tell us that while God does expect us to speak when appropriate, He values silence – and what's good enough for God is certainly good enough for us.

Dear God,
Help me to remember
that silence is indeed
golden. Bless me with the
wisdom to know when to
speak and when to stay
quiet.
Amen

18

Righteousness

A gift opens the way for the giver and ushers him into the presence of the great.

Proverbs 18:16

A lot of people think that businesses contribute to charities and community programs to get the tax deduction. While the tax deduction is appreciated, I doubt that it's one of the top motivations – if for no other reason than the tax deduction is only a fraction of what was donated.

In most cases, the giving practices of a company directly reflect the values of its leaders – just as the giving practices of individuals reflect their own personal values and commitments. You can tell a lot about a company just by looking at its philanthropic policies.

I used to work for a company that supported the United Way. Nothing wrong with that – except the company's goal was 100 percent participation in the United Way's Fair Share campaign. I had a serious problem with that.

First, the "fair share" amount was one hour's pay per month. While that might not sound like a lot, I was young and struggling to make it on my own, and every penny counted. Second, I am an admitted control freak, and I didn't like the idea that I would give my money to the United Way and someone on the agency's staff would make the decision about what charities to pass my contribution along to. Third, I didn't see the logic behind having the United Way as a "middleman" – I thought people could make their own donations as they were so inclined, without funneling the funds through a third party. Fourth, and probably most important, I resented the pressure from my coworkers and managers to "donate" in this way – and the pressure was intense.

The Bible has a lot to say about giving – not just giving money, but also giving tangible items and services (food, clothing, shelter), and through those gifts, demonstrating our love for God and the recipients.

True Christian giving is done freely, voluntarily and cheerfully. It is driven by the heart, not by fear, not by threats, and certainly not by the promise of a reward. When we give as God tells us, we please God. And when we please God, we are drawn closer to Him.

Dear God,
Guide me to give
according to Your will, to
be Your instrument in this
world where the need is
so great. Accept my
meager gifts and multiply
them in Your service.
Amen

19

Purpose

Many are the plans in a man's heart, but it is the Lord's purpose that prevails.

Proverbs 19:21

Most job candidates would agree that "Where do you see yourself in five years?" is among the top three annoying and frustrating questions they are asked.

The vast majority of us are lucky to have a reasonable idea of what we're going to be doing next month – but five years from now? All I know for sure is that if I'm still alive in five years, I'll be five years older. We may have plans, but life gets in the way. Things happen that we didn't expect. And all too often, what we think we want and what we build our plans around aren't what God has in mind. That's when our plans change.

This is not to suggest that we shouldn't plan. We absolutely should. We are made in God's image, and God is the ultimate long-range planner. The difference, of course, is that His plan is final. That's why God doesn't have a Plan B – He doesn't need one.

Still, even though He clearly has the advantage when it comes to planning, He wants us to set goals and make plans to reach those goals. More important is that He wants to be involved in the process – and when He is, putting together your plan gets a lot easier. To pursue a plan that is not in line with God's purpose for us – no matter how great you think it is – is a waste of time and effort.

Don't try to sell your plans to God; instead, ask God what He wants you to do and make that your plan. Listen for God's will before acting on your plans.

Dear God,
I have a lot of ideas, a lot
of plans. There are so
many things I want to do.
Most important is that I
want to please You. Thank
you for keeping me on
track, living and working
according to Your purpose
for my life.
Amen

20

Forgiveness

Do not say, "I'll pay you back for this wrong!"
Wait for the Lord, and he will deliver you.

Proverbs 20:22

I t's been said that living well is the best revenge – and maybe it is. But someone with a vengeful heart and mind can't live well because they haven't been able to let go of the hurt and bitterness that is slowly poisoning them.

The desire for retribution is a human response to what psychologists call a narcissistic injury, essentially a wounded ego. Taking revenge is little more than responding to evil with evil. While there might be times when it is appropriate to fight fire with fire (especially in the case of an actual fire), we should never respond to evil with evil. Instead, we should respond to evil with good – deep, genuine love and kindness.

If someone speaks badly about you behind your back, praise them publicly.

If someone is cool and distant to you, be warm and friendly to them.

If someone hurts you, do something designed to make them feel good.

Do you see the pattern here? Revenge comes at a price and rarely brings the expected results. You think getting revenge will make you feel better, but it doesn't. Revenge is the hurtful side of reciprocity. It's primitive and destructive.

So is living well really the best revenge? Perhaps, but if you are truly living well, you aren't seeking revenge. You release your anger and pain, you take the proverbial high road, and you pray for the person who harmed you.

Depending on the degree to which you were injured, you may have to go through this process of rejecting the desire for revenge over and over – and that's okay. It gets a little easier each time you do it.

The best revenge is no revenge. The best revenge is found in forgiveness, in letting go and trusting God to be the perfect judge that He is.

Dear God,

It is easy to respond to sin

with sin, to seek revenge

for a wrong done to us.

Thank You for the

strength to resist the

temptation of revenge.

Amen

21

Preparation

The plans of the diligent lead to profit as surely as haste leads to poverty.

Proverbs 21:5

A former client of mine was an attorney who wanted a ghostwriter to produce a series of small books on what people should do in various legal situations. After he first contacted me, I sent him a proposal that described my fees and terms, including the fact that I insist on getting a portion of my fee in advance before beginning work.

His response to the proposal was: "Let's do it" and he sent me a check.

Sounds good, right? Well, no. My usual policy when the proposal is accepted is to create a letter of agreement based on the proposal that adds a number of housekeeping items, such as when payments are due and what happens if the scope of the project changes. While it occurred to me that I should slow down and take the time to create and get him to sign a written agreement, I told myself that the proposal was sufficient, I had his initial payment and it was safe to move forward.

I was wrong. He wanted far more work than I had proposed but he didn't want to pay for it. I don't think he was intentionally trying to cheat me; I think he didn't understand what was involved. So instead of creating a series of books that would have been profitable for me and generated business for him, we got the first manuscript completed months after the target date and then ended up in litigation. I sued him for non-payment; he threatened to sue me for a bunch of things. We settled out of court for an amount that was less than I felt I should have gotten and more than he felt he should have had to pay.

If I hadn't rushed, if I had followed my own procedure and insisted on the letter of agreement, things probably would have turned out far differently. Instead, we both lost. The lesson: Don't hurry into projects or agreements without sufficient preparation.

In retrospect, I realize that the little voice in the back of my mind that was saying, "Do the letter of agreement" was God talking – and my decision to do without it was me thinking I knew better.

When you get that nagging feeling to slow down, stop and ask God if He's trying to tell you something. Chances are, He is.

Dear God,

It's not always easy to understand and accept Your time. Thank you for your patience in reminding me over and over to listen not just for Your will, but for Your guidance as well.

Amen

22

Power

Rich and poor have this in common: the Lord is the Maker of them all.

Proverbs 22:2

Two young job applicants were sitting in the reception area of a company, waiting to be interviewed for the same job, when a shabbily dressed man approached the building carrying a large, obviously heavy box. The applicants could clearly see the man through the glass door and windows.

The first applicant was making small talk with the receptionist, and when he saw the man struggling with the door, he remarked, "They really ought to give these guys carts – and make them wear uniforms." He didn't leave his seat.

The second applicant jumped up and opened the door for the man. As the man crossed the lobby, obviously headed for another closed door, that applicant said, "Wait, let me get that door for you." The man expressed his thanks and disappeared down a hallway.

A few minutes later, the human resources director stepped into the room. She was a well-dressed woman both applicants had met before, and they came to their feet when they saw her. She approached the first applicant and said, "Thank you for coming in. We appreciate your interest in our company, but the position has been filled."

As the first applicant left the building, the second moved as if to follow but was stopped by signal from the HR director. After the first applicant was out of sight, she smiled and said, "We'd be honored if you would join our team. When can you start?"

Confused, the second applicant said, "I don't understand. I thought I needed to go through another interview – and you just said the job had been filled."

"I admit I wasn't completely honest about that," she answered. "I should have said that I was hoping to fill the position with someone else – you." After a short pause, she continued, "There was a man who came through the door carrying a heavy box. You held the door for him and offered to help in again when he had to go through another door." She said nothing about what the other applicant had done; she didn't need to. "You demonstrated the kind of character we want in our employees."

"How did you know about that?" the applicant asked.

"The man you helped is the president of our company."

It's been said that the true measure of a person's character is how they treat someone who can't help them, whose job is to serve them or who ranks below them on some manmade hierarchy. We cannot elevate ourselves by degrading others. From the lowliest janitor to the most senior executive, we are all God's children and all the same in His eyes.

Dear God,
Every day You give me the
opportunity to serve
others and, in doing that,
to serve You. Thank you
for keeping me alert to
these chances to live Your
Word.
Amen

23

Abundance

Do not wear yourself out to get rich; have the wisdom to show restraint.

Proverbs 23:4

Many years ago, a then-business partner and friend asked me to pick up her son from his kindergarten class and take him to meet his first grade teacher. Though this event had been on her calendar for several weeks, she couldn't go, she said, because she had an important client meeting that could result in a lot of revenue for us and her husband couldn't get away from his job, either. When I suggested rescheduling the meeting, she assured me that wasn't possible, that the client was demanding a meeting at this exact time.

Reluctantly, I agreed to her request. As I did the best I could at being a stand-in for a sweet youngster's frequently MIA parents, I wondered if it bothered them that they were missing so many of their child's important "firsts" – the first time he saw his first grade classroom, the first time he met his teacher (and how he so politely shook her hand), the first time he sat at his "real school" desk.

My business and personal relationship with this woman eventually disintegrated. We had some great professional synergy when it came to creative work, but our priorities were just too different. She routinely committed to projects and deadlines that required working 20 hours a day to meet. I don't mind doing that occasionally when there's a valid reason for it, but I don't want to work that way on a regular basis.

In retrospect, I should have refused her request that day and insisted that she put her son ahead of making money. I think if she had told the client she was unavailable and offered an alternative when he first requested the meeting, he would have agreed without a second thought.

Of course, I can't do it over, and I'm not going to spend time and energy regretting something I can't change. What I can do is remember the lesson: Business and money are not the most important things in the world. We will enjoy our work and the fruits of our labors more if we don't work to the point of exhaustion and to the exclusion of all else.

God rested after He created the world. Jesus carved out time to rest and to spend with the people who were especially important to Him. If they did it, shouldn't we?

Dear God,

It's easy to get so wrapped up in working and making money that we forget what's really important. Thank You for reminding me – sometimes over and over! – to prioritize my life according to Your will.

Amen

24

Honor

Do not gloat when your enemy falls; when he
stumbles, do not let your heart rejoice

Proverbs 24:17

Competition is key to making a capitalist system work, and we should be happy when we outperform our business competitors and reap the rewards. Sometimes, though, we have the opportunity to reap rewards we didn't earn. What's the right thing to do when that happens?

During the 2001 Tour de France, contenders Lance Armstrong and Jan Ullrich were fighting for the lead in the world-famous bicycle race when Ullrich crashed. Armstrong could have taken advantage of the time it took Ullrich to recover, but he didn't. He slowed and waited for Ullrich to get back on the road. Armstrong went on to win – but he did it fairly.

Two years later, the tables were turned. Again in a battle for the lead with Ullrich, Armstrong crashed when a spectator caught the handlebar of his bike. Ullrich could have taken advantage of the opportunity to gain significant time over his rival, but he didn't. He waited for Armstrong to get back in the race – a race Armstrong went on to finish in first place, but both he and Ullrich were winners for their demonstrations of fair play and integrity.

Will your company gain customers because a competitor made a mistake? Sure. Could your own career benefit because of someone else's failure or misfortune? Of course. And it's hard not to feel a sense of satisfaction when someone whose own ethics and tactics are less than honorable gets taken down a peg or two. But resist those feelings. God doesn't want us to judge, nor does He want us to celebrate someone else's misfortune.

Do the right thing, pray for your enemies, and trust in the Lord.

Dear God,

Thank You for the wonderful plan You have for me – even though I don't always understand how that plan is working. Forgive me for taking pleasure in anyone else's misfortune and help me to focus on what You would have me feel and do.

Amen

25

Sincerity

Like clouds and wind without rain is a man
who boasts of gifts he does not give.

Proverbs 25:14

❝Let me check on that and call you back."
But the call back never comes.

"I'll take that charge off your bill." But next month, the charge is still there – with interest and a late fee added.

"We'll be there to do the job at 9 a.m. Tuesday." But when they haven't shown by after lunch and you call, you get a breezy, "Sorry, they're running late. We'll have to make it Thursday." Or maybe never.

"You did such a great job, I'm going to tell your boss." But the boss is never told.

If you asked any of the people who said those things if they thought keeping promises was important, they would likely respond yes. And maybe they don't see broken commitments in the workplace as broken promises – but that's exactly what they are.

Sometimes there are valid reasons why people don't do something they said they would. Maybe they were depending on someone else who dropped the ball or something else stopped them from following through. Sometimes it's an honest mistake. Maybe they didn't know what they said they'd do wasn't possible or they just forgot.

And sometimes they simply had no intention of keeping their promise in the first place.

God never drops the ball, He never forgets – and He always keeps His promises. He's the perfect role model for our relationships with our coworkers and customers.

Dear God,
Thank You for making
your promises perfectly
clear and for never failing
to keep them. I know
what to expect from You,
and You never let me
down. Please help me live
up to Your example.

Amen

26

Kindness

*Like a madman shooting firebrands or deadly
arrows is a man who deceives his neighbor and
says, "I was only joking!"*

Proverbs 26:18-19

" What's the matter? Can't you take a
joke?"

How many times have those words been used to excuse ugly,
insulting, hateful remarks that should never have even been
thought, much less spoken?

Certainly a sense of humor makes getting through life a lot
easier – especially if you're able to laugh at yourself. God wants us

to laugh, to be cheerful and joyful. But jokes made at anyone else's expense aren't funny. In fact, they're not really jokes.

The occasional good chuckle can make your workday more pleasant and maybe even diffuse a difficult situation with a colleague or customer. Unfortunately, so much of what passes for entertainment in today's world has desensitized us to the difference between genuine amusement and hurtful, offensive messages. We need to learn discrimination in the highest sense by developing the ability to differentiate between real wit and poorly-disguised attacks.

We should never try to mask with humor something we wouldn't say seriously. And we shouldn't pretend to be amused when we are actually offended. We need to quietly but firmly make our feelings known.

Can you take a joke? Sure – if it's really a joke.

Dear God,
Thank You for the gift of
laughter. Please guide my
thoughts and words so
that my attempts at
humor will always be
worthy of You.
Amen

27

Praise

Let another praise you, and not your own mouth; someone else, and not your own lips.

Proverbs 27:2

One of the best things about online shopping and the internet is the ability to share information with other consumers through product reviews. Of course any company is going to tell you how great their product is, but it's more believable when that information comes from a customer.

If you're not doing this already, include customer testimonials and specific product reviews in your online and offline marketing materials. When asking for testimonials, encourage your customers to be specific, benefit-focused and outcome-driven. Those are the endorsements that drive sales.

What about when it comes to your own skills and achievements? Your best strategy is show, don't tell – let others do the talking about your performance. The message will be more believable and far more powerful.

Of course, this doesn't mean you should never claim your accomplishments. There are situations when you need to do that, such as when you're writing your resume or when you are the other person's only source of information. But whenever possible, provide independent confirmation – a believable recommendation from a third party.

When you are in a position to praise someone else, do it honestly and generously.

This is marketing advice that the so-called gurus charge thousands of dollars for, yet you can find it for free in the Bible.

Dear God,

For all that I have and am, I give praise and glory to You. Keep me quiet when I'm tempted to brag about myself and open my lips when I have something nice to say about someone else.

Amen

28

Vision

He who works his land will have abundant
food, but the one who chases fantasies will have
his fill of poverty.

Proverbs 28:19

Years ago, it was known as the seminar industry: a business that was populated by companies that marketed through late-night infomercials and sold products (sometimes books and audio tapes, then eventually CDs and DVDS, and sometimes classroom training) through seminars typically held in hotels around the country. That business model has evolved and is now referred to as the information products industry. Companies still hold seminars in hotels, but they also sell through teleseminars, webinars, online video and audio, and more.

The seminar industry had a well-deserved sleazy reputation with more than its share of rip-off artists, and eventually consumer protection agencies took aggressive action against the worst offenders. However, to be fair, many of the products contained legitimate information that, if properly learned and consistently executed, would generate positive results. But even the companies selling those products deliberately targeted people who weren't likely to follow through – but who were likely to buy again. And again.

Today's information products industry depends on customers known as "opportunity seekers" – people who are always looking for that next idea, that next business, that next get-rich scheme that's "really going to work this time." The problem is that most of these people are chasing fantasies. In their quest for quick and easy success, they aren't realistic, they don't stay focused and they don't do the work.

God wants us to dream – and dream big! He wants us to turn those dreams into goals, develop a plan to reach those goals, and use our gifts to create abundance for ourselves and others. But while He promised it would be possible, He didn't promise it would be easy – or quick.

Ask God to show you His plan for you and then work the plan.

Dear God,
You want more for Your
children than we can
imagine. I pray for the
vision to see
opportunities clearly and
the wisdom to make
decisions according to
Your will.
Amen

29

Truth

If a ruler listens to lies, all his officials become wicked

Proverbs 29:12

I had been discussing some possible new projects with a former client of mine when he invited me to sit in on a meeting that was supposed to be a brainstorming session with his key advisors. My client, who owned the company, immediately began dominating the conversation. When others tried to speak, he just talked louder. Finally he paused long enough for one of the advisors to say firmly, "I think you're wrong, and here's why."

But before the advisor could offer his perspective, the owner interrupted, saying that it was his company, his products, his customers and he knew best. The advisor listened, then again tried to share his opinion, this time with a little more forcefulness (and some frustration) in his voice.

The owner went from speaking loudly to shouting, repeating his previous assertions, and finally telling the advisor that if he disagreed, he could leave.

The advisor sat quietly for the rest of the meeting, while two others expressed their agreement with the owner. I was grateful that no one asked for my opinion, because I agreed with the advisor who had been shouted down. The meeting ended on a stiff, awkward note.

The project that was being discussed never got off the ground.

The client and I never came to terms on the projects we had been discussing. I heard that the advisor eventually dissolved his business relationships with the company and my former client.

Regardless of your position within an organization, always surround yourself with people who will tell you not just what you want to hear, but the truth – and listen to them. When you are in the position of advising, offer only the truth – don't lie just because that's what the boss wants to hear. Even if you end up paying a short-term price for your honesty, the long-term gain will be worth it.

Dear God,

You are the Truth. Grant me the strength to be a consistent reflection of Your integrity, no matter what the earthly price.

Amen

30

Stewardship

Ants are creatures of little strength, yet they store up their food in the summer

Proverbs 30: 25

While God gave us dominion over the Earth and everything on it, He also created a world full of lessons from the very creatures for whom we are responsible. The seasons of the year match the seasons of our lives. Birds that sit on their eggs, nurture their hatchlings, teach their young to fly and then kick them out of the nest show us how to be parents. We can learn about community and sharing from animals that live in various types of packs. And the animals that store food for the times when fresh meals will be scarce teach us about saving.

God wants us to be good stewards in all aspects of our lives – personally as well as in our churches, communities and workplaces.

For employees, this means treating the company's resources with the same respect and concern you give your own. Don't fall victim to the attitude of "the company is paying for it, so I don't care." If the company is paying you, you should care.

For employers, this means allocating resources in a way that accomplishes an efficient, profitable business operation while building reserves (saving) and designating a portion of the company's revenue for charity (giving). And if you want to develop programs that encourage workers to serve others outside the company, even better.

Good stewardship is not just personal. It's not a sometimes thing. It's all the time, everywhere, in everything we do.

Dear God,
Thank You for the
opportunity to care for
Your creation. Help me to
always be a good steward
of Your gifts.
Amen

31

Victory

Speak up for those who cannot speak for themselves

Proverbs 31:8

A young woman who worked for one of my clients was trying her best to be both independent and financially savvy. She saved her money and bought a classic "fixer-upper" house. She had a small nest egg for emergencies and was having fun working on her new home as she could afford things on her budget. But her savings were wiped out when the cost of an unexpected major repair for her car was followed by the expense of fixing the damage from a leaking pipe. And then her stove broke.

She had a sense of humor about not being able to cook, but one of her coworkers with whom she had developed a close friendship knew she was worried about what might happen next. That person brought the situation to the attention of their mutual manager in the context of "if she's a little distracted, please be patient with her."

The manager did more than that: he mentioned it to the company's owner. And the owner decided to help by arranging and paying for all of her kitchen appliances to be replaced. He did it anonymously and managed to make it a surprise. The only reason I found out about it was I happened to be in his office one day when the logistical details of the installation were being discussed.

Workplaces have a formal and informal hierarchy. The published organizational chart that explains who is officially responsible for what doesn't always track with the informal power structure and how things really get done.

Most of us have more power than we realize. Often that power doesn't come from what we can actually do, but from whom we can influence. When we use our power wisely, for good, to help people, we are using our power as God intended.

Dear God,
You are all-powerful and
any power that I have is a
gift from You. Guide me to
use power according to
Your will and plan.
Amen

Thank You!

Thank you for joining me on this journey through *Proverbs*.

As the writer or ghostwriter of more than 25 business books, 3,000+ articles, and countless ebooks, blogs, white papers and more, I believe that the absolute best business book of all time is *Proverbs*. No matter where we are in the corporate hierarchy, no matter what situation we find ourselves in, the right guidance can be found in Solomon's words.

Please share your thoughts on *Words to Work By*. Visit www.wordstoworkby.com to join the conversation.

Jacquelyn Lynn

P.S. To learn more about the work I do, visit my business website at www.jacquelynlynn.com. You're also invited to check out my personal blog at www.whatjackiethinks.com — that's where I share my thoughts, opinions, rants and whatever else comes to mind.